Unafraid To Die

A Guide of Comfort and Hope for Facing the End of Life

MaryAnn Moore

Trust in *Him* Communications

Unafraid To Die
Copyright © 2008 by MaryAnn Moore

Information requests should be addressed to:
Trust in *Him* Communications, P O Box 5743, Granbury, TX 76049 or email MaryAnn at maryann@unafraidtodie.com

---

ISBN 978-0-6151-8973-4

All scripture quotations are from the King James Version of the Bible. Public Domain.

All rights reserved. No part of this book may be reproduced, stored in a retrieval system, or transmitted in any other form or by any means—electronic, mechanical, photocopy, recording, or in any other-except for brief quotations in printed reviews, without prior permission of the publisher.

In Memory of William L. Shiflett, 1935-2005, whose example of tremendous grace and faith while facing his death set the bar high for all who loved him.

Acknowledgments

I would like to thank God for giving me this mission. And for bringing such wonderful people into my life: Jim Monahan for his unconditional love; Linda Kistner for her unfailing support from the day I was born; Carlene Greaves Goodpasture for showing me through example how to let go of worry; Tom and Janell Kerby for the generous use of their Christian reference library; Rita Ritter for her encouragement when I first described this project, and the Dames for surrounding me with their faith, love, and friendship.

In addition I would like to acknowledge Pastor Robert A. Shelton for his support of our family, Sheldon L. Kenslow for the laughter and light he brought us, and to Robert "Bob" Angle for the effort he went to to make sure Daddy's last taste of life here was sweet.

Philippians 1:3 KJV
I thank my God upon every remembrance of you,

Contents

Introduction	8
You Can Run but You Can't Hide	10
Say Goodbye to the Big Bad Wolf	33
You Didn't Choose Your Birthday Either	53
Bon Voyage Not Goodbye	65
Why Should I Care, I'll be Dead	77
With A Little Help from Your Friends	100
Watching Childbirth Isn't Easy Either	115
A Final Note	142
Appendix	143

If you bought this book for yourself, good for you! Facing that death, whenever it comes, is nothing to be afraid of is both life affirming and freeing.

If someone bought this book for you, they must love you very much. But after reading the title, your first instinct may be to plaster a fake smile on your face, thank them, and then trash it as soon as they are out of sight.

Don't! Your reaction is exactly why they bought you this book and why you need to read it. Facing death isn't going to cause you to die. It's going to help you live. Forever.

Turn the page. I dare you.

This book belongs to:

_____

Introduction

If you or someone you care about is dying, you've probably already been told or read that when faced with death there are set stages you will experience. Initially upon hearing the *bad news* you will promptly stick your head in the sand. This will be followed by shaking your fist at the sky during the anger stage and the I'll never eat chocolate (drink, cuss, smoke, fill in the blank) again if you'll just let me live stage. And finally you will work your way through extreme sadness to the final shoulder shrugging "OK I get it" final step. All of which paints a pretty dreary picture of how we are doomed to spend our final days on earth.

Introduction

Luckily there is another way. How do I know this? I am the reason the term "Daddy's Girl" was invented. Yesterday was the day I have dreaded above all others. Yesterday my father died.

But because I applied the lessons in this book I did not drown in sadness and grief as expected. And, even more importantly, our final months were not wasted on denials or regrets. Instead we were able to face his death together-supporting each other with laughter, love, and an openness to and acceptance of God's perfect plan.

You can do this too. Let me show you.

Proverbs 12:28 KJV
In the way of righteousness is life: and in the pathway thereof there is no death.

1

You Can Run but You Can't Hide

You and I are going to die. Shocking I know, but true. Botox, daily exercise, cholesterol lowering drugs, and mental gymnastics may make us look younger, feel younger, and act younger, but no matter how hard we try to ignore it, the clock ticks on.

Besides just look at any newspaper's obituary section and you will be faced with the fact that youth does not protect you from death. Plenty of young people leave this earth every day. Behind they leave parents, siblings, and friends who loved them, most of whom were totally unprepared for death to come into their lives.

So even if you somehow magically manage to live forever, at some point you are going to be faced with the death of someone you care about. Death will touch you. You cannot avoid that. But as Proverbs 23:7 points out when it says, *"For as he thinketh in his heart, so is he"*, you can change how you think about death, which will change how you feel about it.

Surprisingly the current attitude toward death being a taboo subject is pretty recent. In our great grandparent's day, death was very much a part of life. Back then you were born at home and you died at home surrounded by family members. Death was not seen as a medical crisis to be solved or a mysterious event to be hidden away but as a natural part of the progression of life.

In Victorian days, when they would not have dreamed of discussing sex, articles about happy deaths were not uncommon. Now days we are willing to discuss sex with strangers but not death with our own family. And the concept of a happy death is almost unheard of. Instead we fight against it till every drop of energy, money, and medical knowledge has been spent.

Why? Because our culture preaches that death is awful. Because at the very time when God's promise of ever-lasting-life should give us and all who love us the ultimate comfort, we allow ourselves to forget what He has taught us. Instead we act like atheists. As if we were facing the end instead of a new beginning.

Of course for some this will be true. If you have not accepted Jesus Christ as your personal savior, then death and what follows will be pretty unpleasant to say the least. Contrary to popular culture, hell is much more than just a *bad* word. It's a bad place. Where you will spend eternity is your choice. And don't kid yourself; not making a choice is one.

You can live a good life without God. You can be a decent person without God. But you cannot defeat death without Him. This is His ultimate gift. Yours for the taking.

John 3:16-18 KJV
16For God so loved the world, that he gave his only begotten son, that whosoever believeth in him should not perish, but have everlasting life.

17For God sent not his Son into the world to condemn the world; but that the world through him might be saved.

18He that believeth on him is not condemned: but he that believeth not is condemned already, because he hath not believed in the name of the only begotten Son of God.

Reflections for Strength and Understanding

1. What do I tell myself about death that makes it scary?

2. What would it feel like to live free of this fear?

3. How can I change the way I feel about death by changing the way I think about it using God's promises as my guide?

4. How could admitting that my life here is not going to last forever make me appreciate the time I do have more?

5. Knowing that I can't prepare for what I won't admit, if I am in denial, how does my refusal to accept the inevitable put myself and my family at risk?

6. If I have not accepted Jesus Christ as my personal savior (see Romans 10:9-10 in the God's Guidance section) what do I risk by doing so? What do I risk if I don't?

Besides reading the Bible, what research can I do or who can I talk to to learn more before making this decision? And remember not making a decision is one.

7. If I have accepted Jesus how do I strengthen my faith so that my death feels like a natural transition to be celebrated, not an end to be mourned?

8. If God told me I only had sixty minutes left on this earth, how many of those precious minutes would I choose to spend on worry and fear? How many on faith and family? Why not allot my time that way now?

God's Guidance

2 Peter 1:16 KJV
For we have not followed cunningly devised fables, when we made known unto you the power and coming of our Lord Jesus Christ, but were eyewitnesses of his majesty.

You Can Run but You Can't Hide

1 Corinthians 15:3-7 KJV
3For I delivered unto you first of all that which I also received, how that Christ died for our sins according to the scriptures;

4And that he was buried, and that he rose again the third day according to the scriptures:

5And that he was seen of Cephas, then of the twelve:

6After that, he was seen of above five hundred brethren at once; of whom the greater part remain unto this present, but some are fallen asleep.

7After that, he was seen of James; then of all the apostles.

Romans 10:9-10 KJV
9that if thou shalt confess with thy mouth the Lord Jesus, and shalt believe in thine heart that God hath raised him from the dead, thou shalt be saved.

10For with the heart man believeth unto righteousness; and with the mouth confession is made unto salvation.

John 14:6 KJV
Jesus saith unto him, I am the way, the truth, and the life: no man cometh unto the Father, but by me.

1 John 4:19 KJV
We love him, because he first loved us.

Hebrews 10:29 KJV
Of how much sorer punishment, suppose ye, shall he be thought worthy, who hath trodden under foot the Son of God, and hath counted the blood of the covenant, wherewith he was sanctified, an unholy thing, and hath done despite unto the spirit of grace?

Hebrews 9:27 KJV
And as it is appointed unto men once to die, but after this the judgment:

Ezra 8:22 KJV
For I was ashamed to require of the king a band of soldiers and horsemen to help us against the enemy in the way: because we

had spoken unto the king, saying, the hand of our God is upon all them for good that seek him; but his power and his wrath is against all them that forsake him.

2 Corinthians 5:10 KJV
For we must all appear before the judgment seat of Christ; that every one may receive the things done in his body, according to that he hath done, whether it be good or bad.

Galatians 6:7-8 KJV
7Be not deceived; God is not mocked: for whatsoever a man soweth, that shall he also reap.

8For he that soweth to his flesh shall of the flesh reap corruption; but he that soweth to the Spirit shall of the Spirit reap life everlasting.

John 14:1-3 KJV
1Let not your heart be troubled: ye believe in God, believe also in me.

2In my Father's house are many mansions: if it were not so, I would have told you. I go to prepare a place for you.

3And if I go and prepare a place for you, I will come again, and receive you unto myself: that where I am, there ye may be also.

1 Corinthians 15:26 KJV
The last enemy that shall be destroyed is death.

John 11:25-26 KJV
25Jesus said unto her, I am the resurrection, and the life: he that believeth in me, though he were dead, yet shall he live:

26And whosoever liveth and believeth in me shall never die. Believest thou this?

Psalm 23:6 KJV
Surely goodness and mercy shall follow me all the days of my life: and I will dwell in the house of the LORD for ever.

You Can Run but You Can't Hide

Psalm 121:7 KJV
The LORD shall preserve thee from all evil: he shall preserve thy soul.

Psalm 116:15 KJV
Precious in the sight of the LORD is the death of his saints.

John 6:47 KJV
Verily, verily, I say unto you, He that believeth on me hath everlasting life.

Psalm 25:4 KJV
Shew me thy ways, O Lord; teach me thy paths.

John 3:15 KJV
That whosoever believeth in him should not perish, but have eternal life.

Unafraid To Die

Titus 1:2 KJV
In hope of eternal life, which God, that cannot lie, promised before the world began;

Luke 16:22 KJV
And it came to pass, that the beggar died, and was carried by the angels into Abraham's bosom: the rich man also died, and was buried;

Romans 1:20 KJV
For the invisible things of him from the creation of the world are clearly seen, being understood by the things that are made, even his eternal power and Godhead; so that they are without excuse:

1 John 5:11-14 KJV
Special note: as we pray remember the guidance given us in 14 "*if we ask anything **according to his will**, he heareth us.*" As tempting as it is to demand, beg, or bargain for the outcome we want, instead spend time asking for the wisdom, strength, and faith to do what God wants.

11And this is the record, that God hath given to us eternal life, and this life is in his Son.

12He that hath the Son hath life; and he that hath not the Son of God hath not life.

13These things have I written unto you that believe on the name of the Son of God; that ye may know that ye have eternal life, and that ye may believe on the name of the Son of God.

14And this is the confidence that we have in him, that, if we ask any thing according to his will, he heareth us:

John 20:29 KJV
Jesus saith unto him, Thomas, because thou hast seen me, thou hast believed: blessed are they that have not seen, and yet have believed.

1 Peter 1:8 KJV
Whom having not seen, ye love; in whom, though now ye see him not, yet believing,

ye rejoice with joy unspeakable and full of glory:

Psalm 49:15 KJV
But God will redeem my soul from the power of the grave: for he shall receive me. Selah.

Ephesians 3:19 KJV
And to know the love of Christ, which passeth knowledge, that ye might be filled with all the fulness of God.

John 4:36 KJV
And he that reapeth receiveth wages, and gathereth fruit unto life eternal: that both he that soweth and he that reapeth may rejoice together.

John 3:36 KJV
Special note: as you read this scripture notice that John says "*he that believeth on the son hath everlasting life*"—not will have but

hath—as in right now this instant everlasting life is yours for the asking!

He that believeth on the Son hath everlasting life: and he that believeth not the Son shall not see life; but the wrath of God abideth on him.

John 5:24 KJV—see special note above
Verily, verily, I say unto you, he that heareth my word, and believeth on him that sent me, hath everlasting life, and shall not come into condemnation; but is passed from death unto life.

John 6:40 KJV
And this is the will of him that sent me, that every one which seeth the son, and believeth on him, may have everlasting life: and I will raise him up at the last day.

Unafraid To Die

John 10:28 KJV
And I give unto them eternal life; and they shall never perish, neither shall any man pluck them out of my hand.

Romans 6:23 KJV
For the wages of sin is death; but the gift of God is eternal life through Jesus Christ our Lord.

Romans 15:13 KJV
Now the God of hope fill you with all joy and peace in believing, that ye may abound in hope, through the power of the Holy Ghost.

1 Corinthians 6:14 KJV
And God hath both raised up the Lord, and will also raise up us by his own power.

1 Thessalonians 4:13 KJV
But I would not have you to be ignorant, brethren, concerning them which are

asleep, that ye sorrow not, even as others which have no hope.

2 Timothy 1:10 KJV
But is now made manifest by the appearing of our saviour Jesus Christ, who hath abolished death, and hath brought life and immortality to light through the gospel:

2 Timothy 2:11 KJV
It is a faithful saying: for if we be dead with him, we shall also live with him:

Hebrews 4:13 KJV
Neither is there any creature that is not manifest in his sight: but all things are naked and opened unto the eyes of him with whom we have to do.

Hebrews 10:38 KJV
Now the just shall live by faith: but if any man draw back, my soul shall have no pleasure in him.

Hebrews 11:6 KJV
But without faith it is impossible to please him: for he that cometh to God must believe that he is, and that he is a rewarder of them that diligently seek him.

1 John 2:17 KJV
And the world passeth away, and the lust thereof: but he that doeth the will of God abideth for ever.

1 John 2:25 KJV
And this is the promise that he hath promised us, even eternal life.

Revelation 20:15 KJV
And whosoever was not found written in the book of life was cast into the lake of fire.

1 John 5:13 KJV
These things have I written unto you that believe on the name of the Son of God; that

ye may know that ye have eternal life, and that ye may believe on the name of the Son of God.

1 Corinthians 2:5 KJV
That your faith should not stand in the wisdom of men, but in the power of God.

Unafraid To Die

My Thoughts and Prayers

2

Say Goodbye to the Big Bad Wolf

Just like the Three Little Pigs we are all afraid of something. A snake could slither across my foot and I wouldn't even shudder. But if a mouse scampered across my screened in porch I'd be dialing 911 and demanding a SWAT team take down my house. Stupid I know. But that's the case with most fears. When you think about them they don't make sense. The problem is most of us never think through our fear. We just feel it.

Take the fear of dying. Heck we fear it so much we won't even use the word unless absolutely necessary. Instead we use euphemisms like, "Sheila passed on." "Joe is no longer with us." Or "Bob left me." In fact, I talked with a woman for a good twenty minutes one time under the impression that her husband had up and left her, most probably for some young floozy, when finally it dawned on me that like Elvis, he had really and truly left the building. I'm sure she saw the confusion on my face, but no matter, she just couldn't bring herself to use the word "dead."

Of course the fear of death might make sense for the unbeliever. I wouldn't be too keen on the idea of just turning into dirt either. For many, the Bible is just a group of nice if somewhat delusional stories and is certainly not a guarantee of an afterlife. They like to say that you can't prove that Jesus rose from the dead. And since you can't prove beyond a shadow of a doubt that he did, how can you be absolutely sure that you will?

Well I can't personally prove that the Revolutionary War took place either as I wasn't there. But I don't think anyone would take me seriously if I ran around arguing that the Revolutionary War never took place because there is no *real* evidence, like a modern day video of Paul Revere swinging his lantern, to prove that it did.

Based on eyewitness accounts, paintings depicting events during the Revolutionary War, and the fact that it did indeed change the face of the world, we all agree it happened. With archaeological evidence and over five hundred eyewitness accounts there is more proof for the resurrection of Christ than any other event in history. Better yet, we have God's word. Still even with this clear picture of Jesus' resurrection, sometimes we Christians have a hard time dealing with dying.

Why? Because at the very time when our faith should strengthen us most, we let our culture's overwhelming message of sadness and gloom drown it out. The night of my father's visitation service, person after person, many who were Christians, came up to tell me how sorry they were. With a long face, they would pat my back and ask in a soft voice how I was doing, how I was *really* doing. When I said smiling, though I'd miss him dreadfully, I was also very happy for the wonderful gift he'd just been given, you'd have thought I had gone nuts. Or even worse, was in complete denial.

But all I was trying to do was live my faith. God tells us that heaven is a wondrous place where we will be reunited with our loved ones forever. We will not feel pain or sadness any more. Everything we need will be provided. Just think, no pain, no sadness, never saying goodbye again, surrounded by all the family and friends that have gone before you. Sounds pretty great to me. How could I not want that for my dad? How could I not want that for everyone?

Still, no matter how strong your Christian faith, as you sit here contemplating your own death or that of someone you love, years of subtle messages that death is terrible and sad are hard to overcome. For instance, when you hear someone has died, what is your first thought? If you are like most of us, "I'm so sorry", leaps into your mind. Just try looking at pictures on the obituary page of your local newspaper and not feeling sad for them and their families. But with practice and the support of like-minded believers you can change your thoughts on death from fear to eager anticipation.

How? Take a second to look back on your personal history to the first time you did something a little scary, whether it was childbirth or your very first day of elementary school. Sure you were nervous, as you'd never had this experience before. But weren't you also a little excited?

As you waited for your first baby you probably spent hours choosing a name, hours decorating the nursery, hours wondering what life would be like with this new little one to love. Before your first day of school, you probably got some grown up school clothes, spent time picking out just the right back pack or lunch box, visited your class room, and met your teacher, and spent time imagining how great it would be to be a first grader and not a lowly kindergartner any more.

You heard over and over how exciting and rewarding being a parent was going to be. Parents, grandparents, brothers, and sisters made being a first grader seem really neat and grown up. In both cases, you spent lots of time focusing on the positive side of this new experience that awaited you.

Still as you breathed through final labor pains or walked up the school's sidewalk, big kids rushing all around you, you probably had an *I'm not sure I want to do this* moment. But it was followed quickly by the bliss of holding your newborn or the thrill of sitting at your desk, a first grader at last. Eager anticipation. You couldn't wait to look into your newborn's face. Couldn't wait to be old enough to go to real school. You filled your mind with thoughts about how wonderful it was going to be and it was. You were surrounded by positive messages about how great it was going to be and they were right.

And what did you do with the few negative messages you may have heard during this time. Like the cranky woman who said "boy once you have kids your life is over". Or the big sister who scared you by telling you about how mean your teacher would be. You drowned them out with the positive messages you got from everybody else.

And as Christians that's what we need to do. Replace our culture's message of fear of death to that of eager anticipation of being reunited with God. Replaying positive thoughts over and over and over in our minds until our reunion with God is so real that we can feel the warmth of His arms as He hugs us in welcome.

What He has planned for us as we open our eyes on the other side of this life is so much greater than becoming a first grader, greeting our first child, or any other life experience we have ever had. He tells us over and over how wonderful our next life is going to be compared to here. He tells us over and over not to fear, that we are in His hands, that He will never forsake us.

Death is His way of bringing us to Him. How can it possibly make sense to fear such a wondrous gift?

2 Timothy 1:7 KJV
For God hath not given us the spirit of fear; but of power, and of love, and of a sound mind.

Reflections for Strength and Understanding

1. Until it becomes natural, I will practice thinking joyful thoughts rather than sad ones when I look at the faces in the local obituaries, knowing that some accepted Jesus Christ as their personal savior and are now celebrating in God's house.

2. To help myself and others, I will write down several positive statements I can use when talking about the fact that I am dying or when talking about the imminent death of a loved one.

3. To help myself focus on eager anticipation rather than fear, I will write down a list of loved ones who have died before me and spend a little time each day vividly imagining what our next meeting will be like.

4. On the days when I feel spiritually weak, I will remind myself of all the other things I do based on faith not facts. For example, do you take herbal supplements? Many have not been proven to work but we spend millions on them just in case they might. Have you ever flown on an airplane? Bet like me you have no real idea how something that huge stays in the air but you board anyway.

5. From the day I was born God has had both a plan and a purpose for me. Any time I catch myself worrying I will stop and remind myself that *He knows what He is doing.* I will have absolute confidence that He will give me what I need to get through whatever He has planned for me. My faith and trust in Him will make me a non-worrier so I can fill whatever time I have left focusing on other people and fulfilling my God given purpose.

6. I will spend some time each day imagining what my first meeting with Jesus and God will be like and keep a running list of things I want to remember to thank them for when I see them.

7. I will remember to talk to God throughout the day, knowing He is

always near to hear my thoughts, to strengthen my faith, to comfort me, and to support me with His love.

8. When I catch myself worrying about the details of what's to come I will stop and remind myself that I am not my body. My body may be sick and dying but my soul is fine. I will learn to separate the two by picturing my body as a great car that has served its purpose. Where once it was shiny and new, now its oil leaks, rusted fenders, and bald tires may mean it's time for the recycle yard. But that doesn't have anything to do with me—because just as my old junker heads into the compactor, I'm jumping out for the ride of my life.

God's Guidance

Psalm 27:1 KJV
The LORD is my light and my salvation; whom shall I fear? The LORD is the strength of my life; of whom shall I be afraid?

Proverbs 3:5-6 KJV
5Trust in the LORD with all thine heart; and lean not unto thine own understanding.

6In all thy ways acknowledge him: and he shall direct thy path.

Psalm 34:4 KJV
I sought the LORD, and he heard me, and delivered me from all my fears.

2 Corinthians 5:7 KJV
For we walk by faith, not by sight:

Hebrews 2: 15 KJV
And deliver them who through fear of death were all their lifetime subject to bondage.

Say Goodbye to the Big Bad Wolf

Philippians 1:21 KJV
For to me to live is Christ, and to die is gain.

Genesis 15:1 KJV
After these things the word of the LORD came unto Abram in a vision, saying, Fear not, Abram: I am thy shield, and thy exceeding great reward.

1 Chronicles 28:20 KJV
And David said to Solomon his son, Be strong and of good courage, and do it: fear not, nor be dismayed: for the LORD God, even my God, will be with thee; he will not fail thee, nor forsake thee, until thou hast finished all the work for the service of the house of the LORD.

Hebrews 13:5-6 KJV
5Let your conversation be without covetousness; and be content with such things as ye have: for he hath said, I will never leave thee, nor forsake thee.

6So that we may boldly say, The Lord is my helper, and I will not fear what man shall do unto me.

Psalm 23:4 KJV
Yea, though I walk through the valley of the shadow of death, I will fear no evil: for thou art with me; thy rod and thy staff they comfort me.

John 14:27 KJV
Peace I leave with you, my peace I give unto you: not as the world giveth, give I unto you. Let not your heart be troubled, neither let it be afraid.

Proverbs 17:22 KJV
A merry heart doeth good like a medicine: but a broken spirit drieth the bones.

Isaiah 32:17 KJV
And the work of righteousness shall be peace; and the effect of righteousness quietness and assurance forever.

1 Corinthians 15:44 KJV
It is sown a natural body; it is raised a spiritual body. There is a natural body, and there is a spiritual body.

1 Corinthians 15:49 KJV
And as we have borne the image of the earthy, we shall also bear the image of the heavenly.

Isaiah 41:10 KJV
Fear thou not; for I am with thee: be not dismayed; for I am thy God: I will strengthen thee; yea, I will help thee; yea, I will uphold thee with the right hand of my righteousness.

Psalm 18:30 KJV
As for God, his way is perfect: the word of the LORD is tried: he is a buckler to all those that trust in him.

Unafraid To Die

Psalm 48:14 KJV
For this God is our God for ever and ever: he will be our guide even unto death.

1 Peter 5:6-7 KJV
6Humble yourselves therefore under the mighty hand of God, that he may exalt you in due time:

7Casting all your care upon him; for he careth for you.

2 Timothy 4:17 KJV
Notwithstanding the Lord stood with me, and strengthened me...

Nahum 1:7 KJV
The LORD is good, a strong hold in the day of trouble; and he knoweth them that trust in him.

Psalm 37:39 KJV
But the salvation of the righteous is of the LORD: he is their strength in the time of trouble.

Mark 4:38-40 KJV
38And he was in the hinder part of the ship, asleep on a pillow: and they awake him, and say unto him, Master, carest thou not that we perish?

39And he arose, and rebuked the wind, and said unto the sea, Peace, be still. And the wind ceased, and there was a great calm.

40And he said unto them, Why are ye so fearful? how is it that ye have no faith?

Proverbs 3:24 KJV
When thou liest down, thou shalt not be afraid: yea, thou shalt lie down, and thy sleep shall be sweet.

Unafraid To Die

Isaiah 41:13 KJV
For I the LORD thy God will hold thy right hand, saying unto thee, Fear not; I will help thee.

Psalm 112:7 KJV
He shall not be afraid of evil tidings: his heart is fixed, trusting in the LORD.

Romans 8:28 KJV
And we know that all things work together for good to them that love God, to them who are the called according to his purpose.

Romans 4:20-21 KJV
20He staggered not at the promise of God through unbelief; but was strong in faith, giving glory to God;

21And being fully persuaded that, what he had promised, he was able also to perform.

Ephesians 4:23 KJV
And be renewed in the spirit of your mind;

Hebrews 11:1 KJV
Now faith is the substance of things hoped for, the evidence of things not seen.

James 1:12 KJV
Blessed is the man that endureth temptation: for when he is tried, he shall receive the crown of life, which the Lord hath promised to them that love him.

Jude 1:21 KJV
Keep yourselves in the love of God, looking for the mercy of our Lord Jesus Christ unto eternal life.

Revelation 3:11 KJV
Behold, I come quickly: hold that fast which thou hast, that no man take thy crown.

Unafraid To Die

My Thoughts and Prayers

3

You Didn't Choose Your Birthday Either

Did you pick up this book because a doctor has given you or someone you love an end date? Or do you worry because your family history points to a short life span?

None of that matters. The doctor with the bad news is just giving you an educated guess. Modern medicine and lifestyle changes can greatly impact family history.

Only God knows when he will call you home. Anything else is just a guess.

Just as I did not decide to be born in December, I am not in charge of when I leave this earth. God tells us this in Job 14:5 "*seeing his days are determined, the number of his months are with thee, thou hast appointed his bounds that he cannot pass."*

Think about that for a minute. The very day you were born God had already decided how long you were going to live here. I know of a woman whose doctor put her into hospice as death was near. That was five years ago. On the other hand a hospice nurse told us Daddy would probably last another three weeks. But that wasn't God's plan. Instead of three weeks he lived three days.

We do not need to worry about when our time will come. God has taken that burden off our shoulders. Though He has decided the number of days in our diary, He lets us fill in the pages.

The moments He gives us are our pen. If you've gotten bad news today, He'll let you waste today's page writing about how scared you are and asking Him "why me" over and over. Or He'll let you fill to-

You Didn't Choose Your Birthday Either

day's page with faith strengthening memories of other times when you could not understand His plan but in looking back you could see now that it too was for your good.

Acts 1:7 KJV
And he said unto them, it is not for you to know the times or the seasons, which the Father hath put in his own power.

Reflections for Strength and Understanding

1. Looking back on my life can I see instances where I did not understand that what was happening could possibly be for my good but now I do?

2. How can I use these examples of the wisdom of God's plan to strengthen my faith and comfort me now?

3. If I have put off making a decision for Jesus till I am old and feeble, absolutely sure, really sick, or have more free time to think about it, how does knowing that my life span is already determined affect my procrastination? Am I willing to bet my soul that I'll beat His deadline?

4. If a doctor has given me an approximate end date, rather than wasting

time feeling sorry for myself, I will view this best guess as a motivational blessing. No longer a procrastinator, I'll get busy checking things off my to do list whether it be mending fences with loved ones, finishing that quilt, or throwing away some of my junk so my family won't have to. What "work" do I still have to be done?

5. A wise woman, after learning that she had breast cancer, spent the first few days being upset and scared. Then she realized she was wasting precious time and switched to a "no matter what lies ahead I'm going to choose to be happy anyway" philosophy. How can you follow her example?

6. How can I use my illness and approaching death to free me from the fears that have kept me from doing things I've always wanted to? Always wanted to sky dive but afraid you'd get hurt? What does it matter now! Always wanted to take a cruise but watched the movie Titanic one too many times? What does it matter now! The clock is ticking. Your time is now. Make Tim McGraw's song "Live Like You Were Dying" your anthem for whatever time is left.

   What is my personal *Live Like You Were Dying* To Do List:

7. What choices do I need to make every day so that whatever time I have left here is used to please both God and me?

God's Guidance

1 Peter 5:10 KJV
But the God of all grace, who hath called us unto his eternal glory by Christ Jesus, after that ye have suffered a while, make you perfect, stablish, strengthen, settle you.

Hebrews 10:36 KJV
For ye have need of patience, that, after ye have done the will of God, ye might receive the promise.

Unafraid To Die

Proverbs 20:24 KJV
Man's goings are of the LORD; how can a man then understand his own way?

Matthew 6:34 KJV
Take therefore no thought for the morrow: for the morrow shall take thought for the things of itself. Sufficient unto the day is the evil thereof.

Luke 12:22-32 KJV
22And he said unto his disciples, Therefore I say unto you, Take no thought for your life, what ye shall eat; neither for the body, what ye shall put on.

23The life is more than meat, and the body is more than raiment.

24Consider the ravens: for they neither sow nor reap; which neither have storehouse nor barn; and God feedeth them: how much more are ye better than the fowls?

25And which of you with taking thought can add to his stature one cubit?

You Didn't Choose Your Birthday Either

26If ye then be not able to do that thing which is least, why take ye thought for the rest?

27Consider the lilies how they grow: they toil not, they spin not; and yet I say unto you, that Solomon in all his glory was not arrayed like one of these.

28If then God so clothe the grass, which is to day in the field, and tomorrow is cast into the oven; how much more will he clothe you, O ye of little faith?

29And seek not ye what ye shall eat, or what ye shall drink, neither be ye of doubtful mind.

30For all these things do the nations of the world seek after: and your Father knoweth that ye have need of these things.

31But rather seek ye the kingdom of God; and all these things shall be added unto you.

32Fear not, little flock; for it is your Father's good pleasure to give you the kingdom.

Psalm 27:14 KJV
Wait on the LORD: be of good courage, and he shall strengthen thine heart: wait, I say, on the LORD.

Ecclesiastes 3:2 KJV
A time to be born, and a time to die; a time to plant, and a time to pluck up that which is planted;

Psalm 139:13-16 KJV
13For thou hast possessed my reins: thou hast covered me in my mother's womb.

14I will praise thee; for I am fearfully and wonderfully made: marvellous are thy works; and that my soul knoweth right well.

15My substance was not hid from thee, when I was made in secret, and curiously wrought in the lowest parts of the earth.

16Thine eyes did see my substance, yet being unperfect; and in thy book all my members were written, which in continuance were fashioned, when as yet there was none of them.

You Didn't Choose Your Birthday Either

Philippians 4:8 KJV
Finally, brethren, whatsoever things are true, whatsoever things are honest, whatsoever things are just, whatsoever things are pure, whatsoever things are lovely, whatsoever things are of good report; if there be any virtue, and if there be any praise, think on these things.

Unafraid To Die

My Thoughts and Prayers

4

Bon Voyage Not Goodbye

But I don't want to leave everybody! When you think about dying, this is probably one of the first reasons *not to* that pops into your mind. It's natural not to want to leave those you love and everything that is familiar. If you've ever moved away from your family or left a job, friends, or a house that was important to you, you've already experienced this.

Of course the big difference was that in those cases you could visit whenever you wanted. Or at least you felt you could. Money might have been too tight or your schedule too hectic to return. But in the back of your mind the thought "If I *really* wanted to I could" comforted you. Death takes that possibility away.

Or at least we think it does. After all Jesus did return to be seen by his disciples. And many people report seeing or feeling the presence of those they love again in times of need. The answer as to whether we will be able to watch over the crib of our great-great grandchildren will remain a mystery until we are on the other side of this life.

What we do know for sure though is that we will be reunited with those Christians we love who have gone before us. And wonderfully once we are with them we will never have to say goodbye again.

It's the time between now and then that most of us struggle with. We look down the long tunnel of years without the people or person we love beside us and think oh how can I possibly stand it? At least that's what I said to myself when I ran the numbers. My math goes like this: 100

(the minimum number of years I plan to live) minus my age the year Daddy died equaled way-way too big a number.

This type of fuzzy math is used by both those left behind and those doing the leaving. If you are leaving you've probably looked at those younger than yourself and thought the same thing. As you go over your mental list, you figure their current ages, how long they are likely to live and ask yourself how can I stand being without them this long?

But remember what we learned in Chapter Three? God decides when we arrive here and when we will leave. I may plan to live to be one hundred. God's plan may be all together different. He may plan for me to join Him and my loved ones much-much sooner. So keeping this in mind it really doesn't make much sense for me to waste time focused on how hard it will be to live without Daddy. Heck for all I know God plans for me to join him this very afternoon. And those grandchildren I adore might be following me in a month or another seventy years.

God has a plan. He doesn't need us to worry about this. How long we will be apart is in His capable hands. The only thing we need to concern ourselves with is helping those we want to join us, through example, teaching, and prayer, turn their lives over to Jesus so they can join Him and us forever.

Genesis 25:8 KJV
Then Abraham gave up the ghost, and died in a good old age, an old man, and full of years; and was gathered to his people.

Reflections for Strength and Understanding

1. How can I use the strengths God has given me to bring those I love to Jesus?

Bon Voyage Not Goodbye

2. Taking a good hard look at myself, what do I do that might turn someone away from believing? And how can I change this behavior?

3. God has given me this opportunity to show unbelievers by example how my Christian faith takes away the fear of death. How can I use this time to help them want to learn more about my faith, and the comfort and promise it gives me?

4. If I catch myself worrying and feeling sad about all those people I will miss, I will immediately replace worthless worry with action. I'll pick up the phone, pen and paper, or my computer keyboard and make plans to spend time with those I love or write them notes sharing special memories and why they mean so much to me. People I need to contact:

God's Guidance

2 Samuel 12:23 KJV
But now he is dead, wherefore should I fast? can I bring him back again? I shall go to him, but he shall not return to me.

1 Corinthians 15:42-44 KJV
42So also is the resurrection of the dead. It is sown in corruption; it is raised in incorruption:

43It is sown in dishonour; it is raised in glory: it is sown in weakness; it is raised in power:

44It is sown a natural body; it is raised a spiritual body. There is a natural body, and there is a spiritual body.

1 Corinthians 15:4-7 KJV
4And that he was buried, and that he rose again the third day according to the scriptures:

5And that he was seen of Cephas, then of the twelve:

6After that, he was seen of above five hundred brethren at once; of whom the greater part remain unto this present, but some are fallen asleep.

7After that, he was seen of James; then of all the apostles.

John 21:12 KJV
Jesus saith unto them, Come and dine. And none of the disciples durst ask him, Who art thou? knowing that it was the Lord.

1 Corinthians 2:9 KJV
But as it is written, Eye hath not seen, nor ear heard, neither have entered into the heart of man, the things which God hath prepared for them that love him.

Matthew 5:16 KJV
Let your light so shine before men, that they may see your good works, and glorify your Father which is in heaven.

Romans 8:37-39 KJV
37Nay, in all these things we are more than conquerors through him that loved us.

38For I am persuaded, that neither death, nor life, nor angels, nor principalities, nor powers, nor things present, nor things to come,

39Nor height, nor depth, nor any other creature, shall be able to separate us from the love of God, which is in Christ Jesus our Lord.

John 8:32 KJV
And ye shall know the truth, and the truth shall make you free.

John 8:51 KJV
Verily, verily, I say unto you, If a man keep my saying, he shall never see death.

Acts 20:24 KJV
But none of these things move me, neither count I my life dear unto myself, so that I

might finish my course with joy, and the ministry, which I have received of the Lord Jesus, to testify the gospel of the grace of God.

Isaiah 64:4 KJV
For since the beginning of the world men have not heard, nor perceived by the ear, neither hath the eye seen, O God, beside thee, what he hath prepared for him that waiteth for him.

Philippians 3:20 KJV
For our conversation is in heaven; from whence also we look for the Saviour, the Lord Jesus Christ:

1 Peter 3:15 KJV
But sanctify the Lord God in your hearts: and be ready always to give an answer to every man that asketh you a reason of the hope that is in you with meekness and fear:

Matthew 22:37 KJV
Jesus said unto him, Thou shalt love the Lord thy God with all thy heart, and with all thy soul, and with all thy mind.

Unafraid To Die

My Thoughts and Prayers

5

Why Should I Care, I'll be Dead

When you think about all the details that are going to have to be taken care of while and when you die, it's tempting isn't it? Taking the *I'll be dead so you can't make me* approach certainly seems easy. You don't have to do the work or come face to face with the details of dying. But what will your avoidance of reality do to those you'll leave behind?

Take a minute right now. Close your eyes and picture the faces of those you love. If you look honestly into their future you'll see the strain of losing you, the confusion about what you wanted for a funeral, the uncertainty and misunderstanding that can tear a family apart when disposing of your estate no matter how small. Is this really the legacy you want to leave them?

God hopes not. In 1 Timothy 5:8, He tells us "*But if any provide not for his own, and especially for those of his own house, he hath denied the faith, and is worse than an infidel.*" In our materialistic society when you see the word provide you may go, "Oh I've got lots of money and neat stuff to leave everybody so I'm OK", or "I've got so little to leave that I've already failed."

But God isn't much interested in the material. What He means is for you to honor your family. And there is no better way for you to do that than to provide them with the final gift of handling your death and the details that ensue in a way that strengthens them, gives them a good example to follow when their time comes, and lifts the decision making burden off them as much as possible.

Now I'm not going to pretend that what I am encouraging you to do is easy. Accepting in the privacy of your head that you or someone you love is dying is tough enough. But once the words are spoken out loud and the details put on paper it all seems so much more painfully real. This is why many people, even in their final stages, choose to avoid any mention of what is actually happening. And sadly often those who see their loved one fading right before their eyes willingly go along with this charade till it is too late.

Though at times it was tempting, I am so grateful that we did not take this path. Instead one afternoon my Dad and I went over his list of pallbearers, which gave him a chance to tell me why this group of buddies was important to him. Another afternoon I helped him write his obituary, which gave me a chance to see in his words what was important in his life. If we had insisted on sticking our heads in the sand, we would not have been able to see these precious opportunities God was giving us to deepen our relationship.

Were my dad and I saints or just particularly tough and insensitive? Heck no. To make it easier for both of us, we used the *just-in-case* approach. How's it work? During all of our discussions dealing with death we'd work in the thought that we probably wouldn't need this information for a while but would talk about it now—"just in case".

While I wrote down the list of cronies he wanted to use as pallbearers, we laughed at some of their ages and how he'd probably get the chance to carry them out first. But I'd write down his list any way, "just in case". When he mentioned he was working on his obituary I joked that I was hoping to do it myself, as I'd always wanted to try my hand at fiction. But I'd take a look at what he came up with "just in case" I ever needed it. And using our just in case approach didn't feel like cheating because, even though the doctors had told us it would be soon, only God knew if soon meant a month or a year.

So no matter how tempted you are to avoid talking about death please, please don't. Looking back I wouldn't give up the memories my dad and I made during those discussions, no matter how tough some of them were, for anything. In fact they are the best gift we ever gave each other.

So what are some of the things you should start working on? It is recommended that all of us near death or not, complete a couple of forms. They are a Healthcare Treatment Directive form and a Durable

Power of Attorney for Health Care Decisions form. A Healthcare Treatment Directive is your written instructions that you want followed if you are unable to communicate your wishes in terms of life sustaining medical treatment. A Durable Power of Attorney for Health Care Decisions is a written statement giving someone of your choosing the power to make health care decisions for you if you are unable to make them for yourself. You can find these forms online, at some doctor's offices and hospitals, through many state governments, and in books written about health directives.

As you fill these forms out you will be asked to choose one person to make decisions for you if the time comes that you cannot make them for yourself. Naturally you will want to discuss your wishes clearly and concisely with this person but it is also important to discuss them with other family members and loved ones, even if they are not in on the decision making process. This way if your decision maker should be called on to make a tough choice, the other people in your circle can give them the support and courage they need to do what they all know you want.

Next take a look at what financial information will be needed. Start by making a list of bank accounts, financial accounts, life insurance policies, monthly income from jobs, social security, veteran's benefits, retirement, and a list of your bills, including mortgages and credit cards. The more information you can put on these lists, like contact names and phone numbers, account numbers, approximate balances, and passwords to access, etc the more helpful they will be.

Also include where you keep your important papers, like your will if you have one, account statements, check books, and the like. Next write down, if you have a safe deposit box, where they will find both the key and the box, keeping in mind that unless their name is also on the box's signature card, it will require extra steps for them to gain access.

Now start on your list of the items you hold dear and who you would like to receive them and why. I know the why takes a little extra time and you may have already told your grandson a hundred times he gets your favorite watch cause it was passed down to you by your grandpa but don't count on folks in stress remembering this. Put it in writing so there is no chance for either misunderstanding, "but hey grandpa told me I got the watch" or just plain old innocent confusion, "wait there are three watches in this drawer, which one belonged to pop's grandpa?"

While it's important to take the time to make a list of items you want passed along to those you care about, it's even better to take a little time to work on an ethical will. Just like a more traditional will, which allows you to share your material possessions, an ethical will gives you a chance to write down and share your life lessons, blessings, history, memories, and what you've learned. Think of it as your chance to share all God has taught you so that future generations can learn from your troubles and triumphs. Seem like a daunting task? There are several online guides to assist you and also books that help you work through the process. Besides think what a treasure you can make for your family out of just a little paper, ink, and time.

At this point you are probably like the kid in the back seat on a long road trip screaming, "Are we done yet!" Sorry no. You've still got your obituary to outline and funeral plans to make. The good news is that you can be as detailed or brief as you want. For your obituary, you can just hit the highlights of your life, birth, marriage, kids, work, and whether you prefer flowers or donations to a favorite charity or go into great detail, keeping in mind that most newspapers charge by the line.

As far as your final party, you can go to the funeral home of choice and choose every detail including your casket, plot, and headstone. Or, at the very least make note of whether you want a visitation, wake, funeral, or memorial service, open or closed casket, what type of clothes and jewelry you want, who should preside, a list of six to eight pallbearers with phone numbers, and any music and readings that you want as part of the service. Also write out a list of people with contact information that you want notified by your family.

Now that you've gathered all this great information what should you do with it? First your doctors, hospital, and the person named in your Healthcare Treatment Directive form and Durable Power of Attorney for Health Care Decisions form should have copies of these completed forms. I also recommend that you keep copies of them in any vehicle you travel in, as you need them at the first sign of a health problem, not twenty miles away tucked in your file cabinet.

You should also keep copies of them, along with all of the other information you have gathered where they can easily be found in your home. Using a bright colored folder or binder will make finding your final wishes/important papers packet especially easy for the person or persons you've put in charge of making sure your wishes are followed

And now we get to the nitty-gritty. Who do you trust to follow your wishes? That is a question only you can answer. But I can advise you, if you are looking at your children or grandchildren, to base your decision on ability and nothing else. Handling an estate, no matter how small, is a job and picking someone who is not up to the task just because they are the oldest, male, or you made a promise thirty years ago is not fair to either them or the rest of your heirs.

And speaking of fairness, when dividing your assets there are two schools of thought. One gives more to those who "need" it. The other splits it evenly. It's yours to do with what you want. I'm just glad when it comes to our inheritance from God, as Peter tells us in Acts 10:34, He treats us all the same.

Genesis 37:3-4 KJV
3Now Israel loved Joseph more than all his children, because he was the son of his old age: and he made him a coat of many colours.

4And when his brethren saw that their father loved him more than all his brethren, they hated him, and could not speak peaceably unto him.

Why Should I Care, I'll be Dead

Reflections for Strength and Understanding

1. How can I use the just-in-case approach to make talking about my death easier on family, my friends, and myself?

2. Who should I ask to be in charge of making health decisions for me should the time come?

3. Have I let my other family members and loved ones know that I have chosen this person as my point person and that he/she will be the central contact for family members and the

one talking to the doctors, hospital staff, hospice, etc?

4. Have I talked openly and clearly with other family members and loved one's about my health care wishes so there will be no confusion about the fact that the person I've asked to be in charge of making these health decisions for me is indeed following my directions? Have I asked them to support and comfort my decision maker if a tough choice has to be made?

5. Who should I ask to be in charge of finding my important papers and following my wishes when the time comes? Would I be more comfortable if I put two people in charge so they can both support and double-check each other?

6. How often do I want to review my final wishes/important papers packet?

7. Have I filled out a new or reviewed my previous:
    a. Healthcare Treatment Directive and Durable Power of Attorney forms and given them to all of the appropriate people. If I need guidance in this area I can contact the Center for Practical

Bioethics, Harzfeld Building, 111 Main St, Suite 500, Kansas City, Missouri 64106-2116, 800-344-3829, www.practicalbioethics.org, for a copy of their excellent booklet called Caring Conversations, which includes these forms.

b. Wishes to be an organ donor.

c. Detailed list of my assets, debts, and passwords.

d. List of where to find my important papers and safe deposit box.

e. List of items I want passed to specific people and why.

f. Ethical Will--for guidance check out the online resources at www.ethicalwill.com, www.yourethicalwill.com, www.alegacytoremember.com, or use one of the many books available.

g. Legal will or trust. Or talked with an attorney, if I don't have one, to see if either might make sense for me.
h. My obituary including whether I want flowers or donations to a favorite charity.

8. Have I made clear my wishes for my funeral, along with a list of people and their contact information that I would like to have notified of the time and date?

9. If I have a spouse what do I need to teach him or her so they can maintain our finances, home, automobiles, laundry, food preparation, social network, etc?

10. If I begin to feel overwhelmed during this process and start throwing myself a pity-party, let me remember that I am one of the lucky ones. By God giving me this notice, I have time to finish my work here; making my departure better for those I love. A quick exit is not an easy one for those left behind.

11. If I am finding it hard or if it is not possible to have the final conversations I want in person, what other options do I have? Can I call, write a letter, or tape a message or have someone help me do so?

12. If I am making a decision that will seem unfair or unclear to those left behind, let me have the courage to explain why to any that may be hurt by my actions.

13. How can I use the conversations I have with family and friends about preparing for the details of my death as visible reminders of my faith in God's plan for me?

14. Have I given the people close to me one on one time so that we have a chance to say what is important to each other in private?

God's Guidance

Philippians 1:20-21 KJV
20According to my earnest expectation and my hope, that in nothing I shall be ashamed, but that with all boldness, as always, so now also Christ shall be magnified

Why Should I Care, I'll be Dead

in my body, whether it be by life, or by death.

21For to me to live is Christ, and to die is gain.

Romans 8:17 KJV
And if children, then heirs; heirs of God, and joint-heirs with Christ; if so be that we suffer with him, that we may be also glorified together.

Titus 3:7 KJV
That being justified by his grace, we should be made heirs according to the hope of eternal life.

1 Peter 1:4 KJV
To an inheritance incorruptible, and undefiled, and that fadeth not away, reserved in heaven for you,

Deuteronomy 33:27 KJV
The eternal God is thy refuge, and underneath are the everlasting arms: and he shall thrust out the enemy from before thee; and shall say, Destroy them.

Jeremiah 6:14 KJV
Special note: you can't heal a wound by saying it's not there. If there is someone you need to make amends to, now is the time.

They have healed also the hurt of the daughter of my people slightly, saying, Peace, peace; when there is no peace.

Isaiah 38:1 KJV
In those days was Hezekiah sick unto death. And Isaiah the prophet the son of Amoz came unto him, and said unto him, Thus saith the LORD, Set thine house in order: for thou shalt die, and not live.

Why Should I Care, I'll be Dead

1 Corinthians 4:2 KJV
Moreover it is required in stewards, that a man be found faithful.

Psalm 73:26 KJV
My flesh and my heart faileth: but God is the strength of my heart, and my portion for ever.

Psalm 62:5-8 KJV
5My soul, wait thou only upon God; for my expectation is from him.

6He only is my rock and my salvation: he is my defence; I shall not be moved.

7In God is my salvation and my glory: the rock of my strength, and my refuge, is in God.

8Trust in him at all times; ye people, pour out your heart before him: God is a refuge for us. Selah

Unafraid To Die

Romans 2:11 KJV
For there is no respect of persons with God.

Psalm 139:23 KJV
Search me, O God, and know my heart: try me, and know my thoughts:

Philippians 2:13 KJV
For it is God which worketh in you both to will and to do of his good pleasure.

1 Timothy 6:6-7 KJV
6But godliness with contentment is great gain.

7For we brought nothing into this world, and it is certain we can carry nothing out.

Why Should I Care, I'll be Dead

My Thoughts and Prayers

6

With A Little Help from Your Friends

Many of us have at one time or another hummed the Beatles lyrics "I get by with a little help from my friends." And now is a good time to take that tune to heart.

There is a reason in the bible God encourages us over and over to help each other. This practice not only strengthens our faith but also humbles us. Problem is, for some of us, admitting we need help can be tough.

With A Little Help from Your Friends

Up till now, you may have lived your life as if asking for help was weak. You probably see your do-it-myself independent streak as an admirable quality. And I'm sure there were times in your life when it was. This is not one of them. During the process of dying, no matter how strong you think you are, you are going to need God. And most likely you'll need lots of other people too, including doctors, nurses, caregivers, family, and friends.

The good news is that while you can, you have the opportunity to maintain some control by gathering information and making plans. A good first step is to talk to your doctors about their best guess estimate of what changes you may face. If they hesitate, remember you have the right to know about your particular illness and the possible outcome you may be facing.

For example, is it likely that you'll need a walker, special feedings, a full time caregiver, or nursing home care? How about a lift-chair that helps you get up or a scooter to help you get around? What kind of assistance can you expect from your local hospice and visiting nurses organizations? How do you make contact with the local people that can help?

Once you get a general idea of what the future may hold, you can come up with a plan. For example, if you may need a walker, what changes in your home would make using one safer? Would eventually removing throw rugs, some furniture, or decorative shelves that stick out in the hallway be a good idea? How about checking into available home health aids, local nursing homes, or hospice facilities just in case that becomes necessary?

Next, once you have a game plan, share this information with those family members and friends who may become involved in your care. This is not the time to be secretive. Keeping the people who mean the most to you out of the loop is neither brave nor strong. Instead your insistence, like a stubborn two year old demanding to *do it themselves* when in reality they can't, is only going to make life harder for you and everyone around you.

Of course talking openly about what may come is not always easy either. When you try to broach the subject, your friends and family may accuse you of being negative or giving up. Remember to use the just-in-case approach we discussed in Chapter 5 to make the conversations a little easier for them. And don't give up. No matter how brief, each conversation makes the next one just a little less hard to handle.

Can't picture taking this kind of control? Had more practice over the years playing the damsel in distress? Then the process of dying may seem the chance of a lifetime to be the center of your family's world. During this time, you can demand that they care for you in your home or theirs no matter how harsh the burden. You can make them jump to your every whim with a gentle reminder of your *condition*. Why with enough practice, you can learn to get your way quicker than a tantrum-throwing toddler.

Of course, as with any bad behavior, there are risks involved in this approach to dying. First this type of selfishness does not please God. And secondly as you head to meet Him, do you really want your family sobbing with relief instead of grief?

So what is the damsel type to do? Easy. Quit thinking about yourself. Just like the do-it-yourselfer, start focusing on how you can use what is happening to strengthen your loved ones' faith and make this natural transition as smooth as possible for both you and them. Gather information. Develop a plan. Share the plan. Make good memories.

Philippians 4:13 KJV
I can do all things through Christ which strengtheneth me.

Reflections for Strength and Understanding

1. Have I made a plan for changes I can expect that will allow me to be prepared for what may come?

2. Have I checked to see what assistance may be available to me when I need it through state programs, my health insurance policies, hospice, the visiting nurses organization, and my church?

3. Though I realize this is the one time in my life when it really can be all about me, me, me, I will make a conscious choice to put me in the shadows and God in the spot light.

4. If in the past I have asked others to make promises to me about my end of life care, realizing this is an unfair

burden, I will release them from these and instead accept God's plan whatever that might be. Even if it means I may have to go where I don't want to, like a nursing home or hospice.

5. I will remember that just because I don't feel well doesn't give me a license to act badly to those around me. I can and will choose to be pleasant anyway!

6. If I am having a tough day, I will alert those around me so they understand and don't feel responsible for my mood.

7. If I am a do-it-yourselfer, I will remind myself that doing less does not make me less. In times of need, accepting help is a strength, not a weakness.

8. I will write down a list of my most uplifting friends and their phone numbers. Then I will make plans with

them to schedule regular chats so that I am constantly strengthened by their light, faith, and laughter.

Name   Number   Schedule

9. If I begin to feel guilty about the affect my illness is having on those who love and care for me, I will remember that I did not choose my situation. God did. As far as I know He is using my illness to teach a lesson, to show by example, or any number of other ways. Instead of feeling guilty, I will trust He knows what He is doing.

10. I will discuss with my loved ones and friends, which I prefer: to be left alone at the very end or to be surrounded by family and friends. If I want my family and/or friends there I will be sure and relieve them of any guilt they might feel if I die while they can't be there or by chance step out

of the room, reminding them that all the other moments we shared are so much more important.

11. If as I talk about my illness with others, they join in with stories of similar cases that are filled with light and encouragement I will soak up their happy message. If on the other hand they begin a horror story, I will gently but quickly interrupt by reminding them that each case is different plus treatments and pain management techniques are improving at such a rapid pace that, in many cases, even last year's story is old news. And for extra measure I'll throw in the old adage that in some ways, and this is one of them, ignorance is bliss.

12. If I am tempted to spare the children in my life from what is happening to me, I will realize that if they are old enough to ask questions they are old enough to get answers. Rather than letting them make up answers in their

imaginations, many of which will be wrong and scary, I will be appropriately open about what is happening to me. And I will view this as an excellent opportunity, through both my words and actions, to teach about faith and how it takes away the fear of death.

13. I will thank God every day for the people He has sent into my life that care about me and care for me.

God's Guidance

Philippians 3:13-14 KJV
13Brethren, I count not myself to have apprehended: but this one thing I do, forgetting those things which are behind, and reaching forth unto those things which are before,

14I press toward the mark for the prize of the high calling of God in Christ Jesus.

Unafraid To Die

Psalm 46:1 KJV
God is our refuge and strength, a very present help in trouble.

2 Corinthians 4:16-18 KJV
16For which cause we faint not; but though our outward man perish, yet the inward man is renewed day by day.

17For our light affliction, which is but for a moment, worketh for us a far more exceeding and eternal weight of glory;

18While we look not at the things which are seen, but at the things which are not seen: for the things which are seen are temporal; but the things which are not seen are eternal.

Isaiah 25:8 KJV
He will swallow up death in victory; and the Lord GOD will wipe away tears from off all faces; and the rebuke of his people shall he take away from off all the earth: for the LORD hath spoken it.

With A Little Help from Your Friends

Psalm 37:37 KJV
Mark the perfect man, and behold the upright: for the end of that man is peace.

Psalm 18:28 KJV
For thou wilt light my candle: the LORD my God will enlighten my darkness.

John 6:63 KJV
It is the spirit that quickeneth; the flesh profiteth nothing: the words that I speak unto you, they are spirit, and they are life.

John 8:12 KJV
Then spake Jesus again unto them, saying, I am the light of the world: he that followeth me shall not walk in darkness, but shall have the light of life.

John 16:33 KJV
These things I have spoken unto you, that in me ye might have peace. In the world ye shall have tribulation: but be of good cheer; I have overcome the world.

Acts 7:59 KJV
And they stoned Stephen, calling upon God, and saying, Lord Jesus, receive my spirit.

Romans 12:12 KJV
Rejoicing in hope; patient in tribulation; continuing instant in prayer;

Philippians 4:19 KJV
But my God shall supply all your need according to his riches in glory by Christ Jesus.

Matthew 6:10 KJV
Thy kingdom come, Thy will be done in earth, as it is in heaven.

2 Timothy 4:6-8 KJV
6 For I am now ready to be offered, and the time of my departure is at hand.

7I have fought a good fight, I have finished my course, I have kept the faith:

8Henceforth there is laid up for me a crown of righteousness, which the Lord, the righteous judge, shall give me at that day: and not to me only, but unto all them also that love his appearing.

John 17:4 KJV
I have glorified thee on the earth: I have finished the work which thou gavest me to do.

Unafraid To Die

My Thoughts and Prayers

7

Watching Childbirth Isn't Easy Either

Coming into this world is not easy. For most of us getting here is a loud, long, messy, painful process. Just ask any mother. And during the birth process, it's not just the mother who suffers. Everyone involved, even those on the fringes, go from nervous to excited and back again. Just ask any grandparent or aunt-to-be. As an observer, since we can't affect the outcome for mother or baby, we do what we can. We offer comfort and encouragement when possible. And we pray.

For most of us, watching someone we love leave this earth will follow much the same process. Sure some folks get lucky and Grandpa, after a meal of his favorite foods with all his loved ones around the table, just goes to sleep in his recliner, never to wake up again. And it's only natural to hope for this perfect ending for those we love. But this is often not God's plan. He may make them suffer. He may make you watch.

Why? Only God can answer that question. But I will tell you that the dying process gives you an excellent chance to strengthen your faith. For some of us this will be the toughest test of our convictions we ever experience, stretching our trust in Him to the breaking point.

But times like these are what faith is for. Anyone can have it when things are going their way. Just like a muscle, you can't really know how strong faith is till it has to carry a heavy load.

Right now, if you are in the first stages of losing a loved one, your faith may feel pretty strong because, before this, you've been walking on flat ground. Once you and your loved one hit a few hills, you may be in for a surprise. As their condition declines, just like a marathon runner, your legs may tremble. Your lungs may ache. Your eyes may tear up from the effort of watching. Reaching the finish line of their death with any sense of sanity may seem impossible.

Though, with God's help you won't actually lose your mind, you won't be the same person when this is over that you were when it started. Losing someone you love makes its mark. The good news is that with God's help you can actually come out of it stronger than when you began.

How? When you find out someone you love is dying first do two things. Number one read the other chapters in this book so you can walk through this process with them. This will not only ease the dying process for them but also help free you of your fear of death.

And number two, and most importantly, place yourself completely in God's capable hands. Admit to Him and yourself that you cannot make it through this experience without Him. Ask Him to stand beside you every step of the way, taking all your worries from you, and carrying you if you fall. He will do this. If you will let Him.

And that's the tough part. Trusting Him enough to leave Him alone to do His will. Because as reality sets in and death becomes imminent, you are going to be really, really tempted to grab back your worries, fears, and control. And if you grab for your troubles, He'll let you have them.

Now I don't know what your favorite fret time is, but when I first learned my dad had brain cancer, I got in the habit of wrestling my worries back from God between about two and three o'clock in the morning. Night after night I'd lay there, sheets twisted, eyes wide open, mind racing, running over and over what I could do, what I should do, and what I had missed that might keep my dad with me till I could stand to lose him.

Then finally one early dawn God whispered in my mind, "and when will that be?" And I realized the answer was never. I was never going to want this. If Daddy was a hundred and fifty, I still wouldn't be ready to let him go.

But God wanted him to come home. And I didn't. So who should win this struggle? Was I wiser than God? Did I have a

Watching Childbirth Isn't Easy Either

better plan than God's? Could I offer my dad a better life here than God could in heaven?

Answering my own questions no, no, and no made it easy to see that to keep my dad here with me when he could be experiencing wonders I can't even imagine, was too selfish even for me. God knows what He is doing.

Trust in this and, instead of wasting time worrying about things you cannot change, you will be free to focus on the precious time you still have left before your loved one leaves you.

How can you best spend this time? Follow their lead. They may just want to sit quietly. They may enjoy a stroll down memory lane. They may want to discuss or have you help them work through some of the things in this book. Or they may just want to feel the touch of your hand gently soothing them.

Just as the other chapters encourage the dying person to talk openly about what is happening to them, I encourage you to do the same. If they bring the topic up, have the courage to listen. Relieving them of the burden of trying to protect you from what is actually happening can be one of the greatest gifts you give them.

But what if they don't bring it up? Should you force the issue? This isn't the time to start a fight. Asking them open ended questions like "How are you feeling about your treatments?" and "How do you feel about all of this?" will help you gauge how open they are to discussing both their feelings and acceptance of their current situation. Then, gently see if you can help them become more comfortable with the subject of dying by talking about some of the things you've learned by reading this book and how this information has changed your approach to facing your own death.

And throughout it all don't forget to celebrate with them both life here and what is coming. Laugh with them at their favorite silly movies on tape or DVD. Call them up and read them some of the great email jokes you've just gotten. Bring over their favorite yummy dessert and pig out, even if it's just a spoonful. Share your favorite bible verses and why they mean so much to you. Talk about what your heavenly reunion might be like. Describe all the silly stuff you both might be able to do in heaven that you can't do here, like pitch a no-hitter against

Watching Childbirth Isn't Easy Either

Babe Ruth or waltz enchantingly with Fred Astaire. Celebrate each and every moment as a precious gift from God.

And after they are in heaven, continue this habit as a tribute to what you learned about life through experiencing their death.

Philippians 4:6-7 KJV
6Be careful for nothing; but in every thing by prayer and supplication with thanksgiving let your requests be made known unto God.

7And the peace of God, which passeth all understanding, shall keep your hearts and minds through Christ Jesus.

Reflections for Strength and Understanding

1. During the dying and grief process, I will remember to concentrate not just on my pain but also on my loved one's amazing gain. Each time I feel my loss and sadness, I will picture them with no pain, no sorrow, having

fun with all the friends and relatives that have gone before, all now in God's amazing home.

2. Using the fact that my mind cannot focus on two thoughts at the same time, I will chase out worthless worry by switching to the here and now. For example, if I catch myself worrying about future troubles, instead of picturing what *might* happen, I will switch my focus to what *is* happening—right this minute. Are birds chirping happily outside the hospital window? How does it feel to softly touch my loved one's skin? Is there a beautiful plant or flower in the room I forgot to notice?

3. Instead of focusing just on me during this process, I will think about how God wants me to impact those He puts in my path during this time, including family members, friends, and

Watching Childbirth Isn't Easy Either

those caring for my loved one. Can my quiet strength of faith during this difficult time strike up the religious curiosity of a family member? While I sit in the waiting room can I help someone else that is alone pass the time and forget their worries for a bit? Can I ease the loss the doctor may feel when nothing else can be done for my loved one?

4. As I interact with those around me, I will remind myself that my actions and words are the visible signs of my faith that others see. Am I a light drawing others to Him or do my actions make my Christian faith appear a fraud?

5. If I am the health care advocate, I will make sure I have all the necessary patient approval clearances so that doctors can talk to me as if I were the patient.

6. If I am the point person for contact with family members, loved ones, the hospital, doctors, hospice, etc, what do I need to do to help insure that I can keep everyone informed? Would a group email, calling circle, or regu-

larly scheduled meetings be the most efficient way to keep in touch?

7. I have read the other chapters in this book and noted areas I can help with, topics I'd like to discuss, and things I should add to my To Do List.

8. If I am the executor of my loved one's estate, what information, papers, and contact information do I need to be gathering?

9. If I am one of the major caregivers for my loved one am I remembering to take care of myself too? If not, whom can I call or what arrangements can I make so that I have time to recharge?

10. During the dying and grief process I will remind myself that being miserable nonstop does not show how much I care and is not what my loved one would want for me. If I catch myself laughing or having a good time I will see it not as a reason to feel guilty but as a gift from God to soothe my pain.

11. No matter how tough I like to think of myself, I will not try to go through this process alone. I will lean not only on God's grace but also on one or two crutch friends who will agree to prop me up with their faith and love anytime, anyplace.
My Crutch Friends List:

12. If I am one of the do-it-yourselfer types talked about in the last chapter, every once in a while I need to stop and ask myself if by insisting on doing everything I am isolating me and my loved one from those who genuinely want to spend time with us and help us.

13. If I am one of the major caregivers for my loved one, have I tried to make sure that the people visiting have had a chance to spend time alone with my loved one so that they can say what is important to each other privately?

14. Have I made sure that I too have said what I want to say to my loved one?

Watching Childbirth Isn't Easy Either

15. If there are children in my loved one's circle of family and friends I will resist the temptation to "protect" them from the dying process. Instead of hiding the truth from them, I will use their natural curiosity as an excellent opportunity to answer their questions and teach them about faith and how it takes away the fear of death. Knowing that the closer the dying person is to their age, the harder it may be to accept, if appropriate, we will also talk about how God has a plan for each of us and knows how long we will need to complete His work. For some of us this may take only ten years. For others a hundred. Either way, when God calls us home our work for Him here is complete. Children in our circle:

16. When my loved one is near the end of their time here, knowing they may subconsciously need my permission, I will love them enough to tell them that I trust God's will and it's OK for them to join Him when they are ready.

17. Just as my loved one, with God's help, did not have to go through set stages of accepting their death, nothing demands that I go through the popularly dictated stages of grief. With God's guidance and sustaining love, I will choose my own path and take my own time.

18. Before memories fade, I will write down treasured moments that happened during this time, like our last conversations, funny stories told, and

special recollections of their visitation, funeral, etc.

19. I will realize that even though my loved one and I are apart for now it does not mean that I have to end my relationship with them. They will continue to be part of my life, till we meet again, through happy stories, great lessons they taught me and good times we shared.

God's Guidance

Revelation 21:3-4 KJV
3And I heard a great voice out of heaven saying, Behold, the tabernacle of God is with men, and he will dwell with them, and they shall be his people, and God himself shall be with them, and be their God.

Unafraid To Die

4And God shall wipe away all tears from their eyes; and there shall be no more death, neither sorrow, nor crying, neither shall there be any more pain: for the former things are passed away.

Matthew 5:4 KJV
Blessed are they that mourn: for they shall be comforted.

Psalm 107:1 KJV
O give thanks unto the LORD, for he is good: for his mercy endureth for ever.

John 14:2-3 KJV
2In my Father's house are many mansions: if it were not so, I would have told you. I go to prepare a place for you.

3And if I go and prepare a place for you, I will come again, and receive you unto myself; that where I am, there ye may be also.

Watching Childbirth Isn't Easy Either

John 14:1 KJV
Let not your heart be troubled: ye believe in God, believe also in me.

Isaiah 41:10 KJV
Fear thou not; for I am with thee: be not dismayed; for I am thy God: I will strengthen thee; yea, I will help thee; yea, I will uphold thee with the right hand of my righteousness.

Psalm 3:3 KJV
But thou, O LORD, art a shield for me; my glory, and the lifter up of mine head.

Mark 5:35-36 KJV
35While he yet spake, there came from the ruler of the synagogue's house certain which said, Thy daughter is dead: why troublest thou the Master any further?

36As soon as Jesus heard the word that was spoken, he saith unto the ruler of the synagogue, Be not afraid, only believe.

Hebrews 4:16 KJV
Let us therefore come boldly unto the throne of grace, that we may obtain mercy, and find grace to help in time of need.

Psalm 9:9-10 KJV
9The LORD also will be a refuge for the oppressed, a refuge in times of trouble.

10And they that know thy name will put their trust in thee: for thou, LORD, hast not forsaken them that seek thee.

Revelation 7:16-17 KJV
16They shall hunger no more, neither thirst any more; neither shall the sun light on them, nor any heat.

17For the Lamb which is in the midst of the throne shall feed them, and shall lead them unto living fountains of waters: and God shall wipe away all tears from their eyes.

Deuteronomy 31:6 KJV
Be strong and of a good courage, fear not, nor be afraid of them: for the LORD thy

Watching Childbirth Isn't Easy Either

God, he it is that doth go with thee; he will not fail thee, nor forsake thee.

Psalm 18:32 KJV
It is God that girdeth me with strength, and maketh my way perfect.

Ephesians 6:10 KJV
Finally, my brethren, be strong in the Lord, and in the power of his might.

Matthew 11:28-30 KJV
28Come unto me, all ye that labour and are heavy laden, and I will give you rest.

29Take my yoke upon you, and learn of me; for I am meek and lowly in heart: and ye shall find rest unto your souls.

30For my yoke is easy, and my burden is light.

Unafraid To Die

Psalm 145:14 KJV
The LORD upholdeth all that fall, and raiseth up all those that be bowed down.

Micah 7:8 KJV
Rejoice not against me, O mine enemy: when I fall, I shall arise; when I sit in darkness, the LORD shall be a light unto me.

2 Corinthians 1:3-4 KJV
3Blessed be God, even the Father of our Lord Jesus Christ, the Father of mercies, and the God of all comfort;

4Who comforteth us in all our tribulation, that we may be able to comfort them which are in any trouble, by the comfort wherewith we ourselves are comforted of God.

Luke 1:37 KJV
For with God nothing shall be impossible.

Psalm 138:7 KJV
Though I walk in the midst of trouble, thou wilt revive me: thou shalt stretch forth thine

Watching Childbirth Isn't Easy Either

hand against the wrath of mine enemies, and thy right hand shall save me.

Psalm 18:2 KJV
The LORD is my rock, and my fortress, and my deliverer; my God, my strength, in whom I will trust; my buckler, and the horn of my salvation, and my high tower.

Psalm 31:24 KJV
Be of good courage, and he shall strengthen your heart, all ye that hope in the LORD.

Isaiah 14:3 KJV
And it shall come to pass in the day that the LORD shall give thee rest from thy sorrow, and from thy fear, and from the hard bondage wherein thou wast made to serve,

Psalm 37:24 KJV
Though he fall, he shall not be utterly cast down: for the LORD upholdeth him with his hand.

Unafraid To Die

Psalm 28:7 KJV
The LORD is my strength and my shield; my heart trusted in him, and I am helped: therefore my heart greatly rejoiceth; and with my song will I praise him.

John 14:18 KJV
I will not leave you comfortless: I will come to you.

Isaiah 58:9 KJV
Then shalt thou call, and the LORD shall answer; thou shalt cry, and he shall say, Here I am.

Psalm 147:3 KJV
He healeth the broken in heart, and bindeth up their wounds.

Romans 5:3-5 KJV
3And not only so, but we glory in tribulations also: knowing that tribulation worketh patience;

4And patience, experience; and experience, hope:

5And hope maketh not ashamed; because the love of God is shed abroad in our hearts by the Holy Ghost which is given unto us.

Romans 15:13 KJV
Now the God of hope fill you with all joy and peace in believing, that ye may abound in hope, through the power of the Holy Ghost.

James 1:2-4 KJV
2My brethren, count it all joy when ye fall into divers temptations;

3Knowing this, that the trying of your faith worketh patience.

4But let patience have her perfect work, that ye may be perfect and entire, wanting nothing.

Revelation 22:20 KJV
He which testifieth these things saith, Surely I come quickly. Amen. Even so, come, Lord Jesus.

1 Thessalonians 5:16-18 KJV
16Rejoice evermore.

17Pray without ceasing.

18In every thing give thanks: for this is the will of God in Christ Jesus concerning you.

Watching Childbirth Isn't Easy Either

My Thoughts and Prayers

A Final Note

Some of you will read this book and think "how unrealistic." And you are absolutely right. Left to our own devices we probably can't pull off twenty to thirty percent of it.

But remember God is both all knowing and all powerful. With Him anything and everything is possible.

Isaiah 40:31 KJV
But they that wait upon the Lord shall renew their strength; they shall mount up with wings as eagle; they shall run, and not be weary; and they shall walk, and not faint.

Appendix

Being able to stand up and speak at my father's funeral was an outward sign of the strength God had blessed me with during this time of trial. Due to the high number of requests I received for a copy of my statement of faith, I am including it here.

Delivered at the Funeral of Lee A. Goodpasture, March 15, 2007

Oh what a miserable day today is.... For the non-believer. For the non-believer Daddy is dust, grandpa is gone, my friend is finished. For the non-believer today is a grief filled final goodbye.

But we believers know better, don't we! We know that today is a day to celebrate a life well lived. Today is a chance to put words into action—faith on display.

Of course it's a lot easier to talk in the abstract about how wonderful heaven is, what a great reward it is to make this final journey, to leave the pain and shackles of this life behind. But when it happens to someone we love, too often those thoughts fly out the door.

But today, right now, let's show God we really believe what He has promised. Let's show Him that we celebrate joyfully the reward my father's been given. Let's laugh and tell great stories about him and talk about how some great day, hopefully far, far from now, we'll join him.

Appendix

God's Guidance Scripture Summary

The Old Testament
Genesis 15:1
Genesis 25:8
Genesis 37:3-4

Deuteronomy 31:6
Deuteronomy 33:27

2 Samuel 12:23

1 Chronicles 28:20

Ezra 8:22

Job 14:5

Psalm 3:3
Psalm 9:9-10
Psalm 18:2
Psalm 18:28
Psalm 18:30
Psalm 18:32
Psalm 23:4
Psalm 23:6
Psalm 25:4

Psalm 27:1
Psalm 27:14
Psalm 28:7
Psalm 31:24
Psalm 34:4
Psalm 37:24
Psalm 37:37
Psalm 37:39
Psalm 46:1
Psalm 48:14
Psalm 49:15
Psalm 62:5-8
Psalm 73:26
Psalm 107:1
Psalm 112:7
Psalm 116:15
Psalm 121:7
Psalm 138:7
Psalm 139:13-16
Psalm 139:23
Psalm 145:14
Psalm 147:3

Proverbs 3:5-6
Proverbs 3:24
Proverbs 12:28
Proverbs 17:22

Proverbs 20:24
Proverbs 23:7

Ecclesiastes 3:2

Isaiah 14:3
Isaiah 25:8
Isaiah 32:17
Isaiah 38:1
Isaiah 40:31
Isaiah 41:10
Isaiah 41:13
Isaiah 58:9
Isaiah 64:4

Jeremiah 6:14

Micah 7:8

Nahum 1:7

The New Testament
Matthew 5:4
Matthew 5:16
Matthew 6:10
Matthew 6:34
Matthew 11:28-30
Matthew 22:37

Mark 4:38-40
Mark 5:35-36

Luke 1:37
Luke 12:22-32
Luke 16:22

John 3:15
John 3:16-18
John 3:36
John 4:36
John 5:24
John 6:40
John 6:47
John 6:63
John 8:12
John 8:32
John 8:51
John 10:28
John 11:25-26

Appendix

John 14:1
John 14:1-3
John 14:2-3
John 14:6
John 14:18
John 14:27
John 16:33
John 17:4
John 20:29
John 21:12

Acts 1:7
Acts 7:59
Acts 10:34
Acts 20:24

Romans 1:20
Romans 2:11
Romans 4:20-21
Romans 5:3-5
Romans 6:23
Romans 8:17
Romans 8:28
Romans 8:37-39
Romans 10:9-10
Romans 12:12
Romans 15:13

1 Corinthians 2:5

1 Corinthians 2:9
1 Corinthians 4:2
1 Corinthians 6:14
1 Corinthians 15:3-7
1 Corinthians 15:4-7
1 Corinthians 15:26
1 Corinthians 15:42-44
1 Corinthians 15:44
1 Corinthians 15:49

2 Corinthians 1:3-4
2 Corinthians 4:16-18
2 Corinthians 5:7
2 Corinthians 5:10

Galatians 6:7-8

Ephesians 3:19
Ephesians 4:23
Ephesians 6:10

Philippians 1:3

Philippians 1:20-21
Philippians 1:21
Philippians 2:13
Philippians 3:20
Philippians 3:13-14
Philippians 4:6-7
Philippians 4:8
Philippians 4:13
Philippians 4:19

1 Thessalonians 4:13
1 Thessalonians 5:16-18

1Timothy 5:8
1Timothy 6:6-7

2 Timothy 1:7
2 Timothy 1:10
2 Timothy 2:11
2 Timothy 4:6-8
2 Timothy 4:17

Titus 1:2
Titus 3:7

Hebrews 2:15
Hebrews 4:13

Hebrews 4:16
Hebrews 9:27
Hebrews 10:29
Hebrews 10:36
Hebrews 10:38
Hebrews 11:1
Hebrews 11:6
Hebrews 13:5-6

James 1:2-4
James 1:12

1 Peter 1:4
1 Peter 1:8
1 Peter 3:15
1 Peter 5:6-7
1 Peter 5:10

2 Peter 1:16

1 John 2:17
1 John 2:25
1 John 4:19
1 John 5:11-14
1 John 5:13

Jude 1:21

Appendix

Revelation 3:11
Revelation 7:16-17
Revelation 20:15
Revelation 21:3-4
Revelation 22:20

My Phone Number and Contact List

Appendix

Not the End

But a New Beginning

www.ingramcontent.com/pod-product-compliance
Lightning Source LLC
Chambersburg PA
CBHW020005050426
42450CB00005B/314